The Garden of My Soul

Let's get digging; have you started the process yet?

Tara Mulumba

The Garden of My Soul

The Garden of My Soul
Let's get digging; have you started the process yet?

Copyright © 2022 by Tara Mulumba

This publication is designed to provide competent information, advice and encouragement regarding the subject matter covered. Scanning, uploading and distributing this book without prior consent from the author is a theft of Intellectual Property (IP).

All rights reserved. No portion of this book without permission may be reproduced, stored in a retrieval system, or transmitted in any form – scanned, electronic, photocopied or recorded without written consent of the author as it is strictly prohibited. Excerpts and links may be used, provided that full and clear credit is given to the author with specific direction and reference to the original content.

If you would like to use material from the book for short quotations or occasional page copying for personal or group study, this is permitted (other than for review purposes). However, prior written permission must be obtained on request by emailing taramulumba1@gmail.com.

The Garden of My Soul

Unless otherwise indicated, scripture quotations are taken from the Holy Bible including the Amplified Bible Classic Edition (AMPC), New International Version (NIV), King James Version (KJV) and New Living Translation (NLT).

Paperback ISBN Number: 978-1-7398998-7-5
e-book ISBN Number: 978-1-7398998-8-2

Published by Authentic Worth
Website: www.authenticworth.com

Authentic Worth is *bringing worth back into you through storytelling and book writing!*

AUTHENTIC
WORTH

The Garden of My Soul

Foreword by Bishop David Onimisi

This book is not just a story, but a life experience of the author. Tara has meticulously written on paper her encounter with the Lord during which He used her garden to paint the picture of the various turmoil's her mind was going through and how to address it. The analogy is actually a clue to the reason why so many destinies are not fulfilled as they get trapped in the pit of past hurts, abuses, betrayals, etc.

Tara emphasises that hiding these feelings behind the facade of drinks and drugs does not bring recovery but prolongs the heartache and consequently leads to a disastrous end. Total recovery is achieved by taking responsibility to address the situation through deep reflection like The Prodigal Son in Luke 15.

Take the time to find out what brought you to the state you're in and resolve to make amends. It's true that you can't undo what you relish, and as long as you keep giving excuses for being where you are, a meaningful change cannot take place. Nothing truly changes until you are willing to change, and the greatest change is YOU because when you change, your perspective changes and you will have a new outlook about people and your surroundings.

This great change that Tara emphasises came when she embraced Jesus as her Lord and Master. The encounter filled the void in her life. Her desire to be loved and valued became a reality. As her hunger

The Garden of My Soul

deepens for the Lord, so her personality which has been trapped in the messy garden begins to be liberated. Her life took a new turn and following the guidance of the Lord, she was able to redeem her past mistakes and turn the mess into a message.

This book is a must read not just for those who possibly might be hurting, but for anyone that truly desires to make the best of living.

Bishop David Onimisi;
Europe Continental Bishop.

The Garden of My Soul

Contribution from Clement Mulumba

When God introduced my wife to me, it was first back in 2004-2005; I am not too sure which year it was exactly. I saw her outside the Nationwide bank with her friends, alongside one of my own friend. I was amazed about her beautiful appearance so much that I decided to enquire more about who she was. My dear friend who was beside her told me she's just a friend and I shouldn't worry about her. Clearly, I could see he liked her too, so I didn't want to get in his way.

I stopped myself in proceeding her, and as far as I was concerned, the case was closed. I had feelings we'd meet again. I can't explain the feelings exactly, but I just knew I would see her again. Years down the line, I saw her walking on the high road pushing a baby pram with a woman that could've been her mother. (I later discovered the woman she walked with was her Godmother).

I was stunted and shocked as I was hoping that one day, we could become more than just *hello and bye distant friends*. I pressed my car horn and waved at her whilst I drove passed. Three years later, I was dropping a friend back home from the gym. While I was driving, my friend took me to the back road. Strangely enough, we saw a woman crossing the road. My friend suddenly realised who the woman was. He hugged me full of excitement while driving saying repeatedly "That's the girl; that's the girl!" I replied

The Garden of My Soul

back; "What do you mean?!" He said "Please talk to her! I know you will be able to break the code." The closer we approached her, I realised who she was. In my heart, I was at peace, and it gave me the courage to approach my wife to be.

The rest is history, and we are here today, happily married with two beautiful children. I have witnessed a brave woman who allowed faith to lead her path. My wife, Tara Mulumba lives her life based on faith. I have seen her take bold decisions and actions and have witnessed the impossible become possible. I am pleased and grateful to God for bringing her into my life.

The Garden of My Soul

Acknowledgements

With special thanks to my Saviour, Jesus Christ, the lifter of my head, my confidante and helper of all things. Where would I be without you? You have pulled me out of darkness into Your marvellous light. All that I've accomplished couldn't be done without You by my side. Jesus, you have been my help in times of trouble; my provider and my comforter. I love you so much!

To my husband, Clement Mulumba; thank you for all the love and support you've given me over the years. We've been through the ups and downs; however, you've supported me throughout. God has used you to hold me up. Thank you for staying by my side in the good and the bad times and for believing in me, my love. You are the best husband ever!

To my daughter Tayah; thank you for your love; the love that you have shown keeps me going. You are God's gift to me. Looking at you gives me strength to push forward to my goals. To my daughter Eden; mummy loves you! Thank you for being you; you bring such joy to me. Your name really does reflect who you are; you are so precious to me.

To my mum; Noella Dowdye, who is the epitome of strength. She raised three kids on her own, always doing the best she could for us. Shout out to my older sister; Tracey Fergus and my younger brother; Andre Williams. Shout out to all my other siblings; Antonia,

The Garden of My Soul

Richard, Fiona and AJ; I love you all. To my auntie Mel, cousin Sandra and family, thank you for always pushing me to be the best version of myself, and even though I may not see you as often as I used to, I'll never forget you always being there when I needed you.

To my Godmother, Tina and Gospel, thank you for always encouraging me. You have stood by me for many years and have been the most amazing Godparents I could ever dream of. Thank you so much for all you do for me and my family.

Thank you so much to Jeanna who started off as a friend to my husband and became a friend of mine also. Thank you for being there and showing up when we needed you. You were there during the birth of Eden and helped when I needed someone to read and critique this book. Thank you for being you and encouraging others to be themselves also.

I want to also acknowledge my dear friend and Reverend, Wonu Adefala who has been a great help for me and has supported me throughout the process and made great sacrifices for me in order for my vision to become a reality.

To my father in the Lord; Bishop David Onimisi; thank you for never giving up on me. You have always seen the best in me. Thank you for allowing God to use you in my life to build me up in God's

The Garden of My Soul

word; always being an open ear for me. Your faith and discipline in God's word is very encouraging to me.

To my mother in the Lord; Reverend Esther Onimisi; thank you for being an inspiration to me. Your great love and humility humbles me; thank you for your encouragement.

The Garden of My Soul

The Purpose of The Garden of My Soul

How long will you desire to change but never do? How long will you be in church and remain the same? There are several issues in our lives that hide under the surface, and if we don't deal with them from the root, they will sprout up and destroy the great works that God desires to bring our way.

The Garden of my Soul aims to bring the reader to a place of reflecting on their own life – to motivate the reader to make concrete changes and deal with the obstacles that prevent them from moving forward.

In this book, I share encounters of what I've gone through to enable the reader to see how past issues affect their future, whilst offering encouragement that it is their responsibility to deal with their own situations. I will be using the analogy of *the garden* to show the reader that addressing every issue in life is a process that will require work. Be ready to get messy!

The Garden of my Soul shows *my own soul*, which is illustrated by the analogy of how a physical garden is cleaned, polished and ready to blossom.

As you read this book, you will come across some diamond symbols. These diamond symbols are key points I want you to take away as they represent those reflection moments.

The Garden of My Soul

Contents Page

Introduction

Chapter 1   1
The Perfect Garden

Chapter 2   8
My Mess

Chapter 3   27
Rodents in the Garden

Chapter 4   45
The Mess

Chapter 5   63
The Turn Around

Chapter 6   73
The Make-Up

Chapter 7   91
Back to Eden

Chapter 8   93
The Message

The Garden of My Soul

Introduction

Many of us have various stories of going through pain and suffering in our lives. Maybe you were abused as a child sexually, physically or emotionally, or you were betrayed by a friend. Maybe you were in love and got hurt or rejected in the process. Whatever the case, if they are not dealt with in the right way, they can result to obstacles in our lives.

Maybe you had repetitive bad experiences with men. Maybe your father was too hard on you, or your ex-partner was abusive, so you've made self-fulfilling prophecies such as "I'll never let no man tell me what to do again!"

After all the bad experiences I had with men throughout the years, I remember saying those words to myself, so by the time my husband came on to the scene, it was hard to hear those famous words of wives to 'submit.' The word 'submit' sounded the same as being a 'doormat' and to me, I was not going to have that, which led to avoidable arguments, stress and a lot of unnecessary tension.

We must be careful about the promises we make to ourselves due to the pain we allow to linger because after a while, those same words and promises we made to ourselves

The Garden of My Soul

can become an obstacle in the future and can bring dysfunction to a blessing.

For example, the arguments in my marriage when I wasn't being submissive could have escalated into more issues, leading to divorce. Thankfully, we both submitted to wise counsel and God's word to address the causes of the issues in our marriage. My husband and I had different challenging life experiences that contributed to how we both responded to each other. These were *'soul-wounds'* that had not been dealt with and had an impact on our lives.

If you live long enough, which if you are reading this book, you have; you will have experienced some negative and traumatic situations that have wounded your soul. We all need to open our eyes to see the effects that the wounds on our souls have on us so we can address them.

Ignoring them will not make it go away no matter how long you ignore them for. Unless you deal with them using the right tools, your heart will not be healed.

I'm not saying, "just get over it," not at all. When I hear phrases such as "let go," or "get over it," I understand why people are offended by these phrases. In the past, whenever I wanted to talk about what hurt me to the people that offended me, or attempted to speak to someone about what I'd gone through, these phrases would come up. It was hard to hear because pain is a real feeling and most people want to let go

The Garden of My Soul

but don't know how to which can lead to frustration. On the other hand, we need to be aware of this dangerous phrase; "I'll never let this go!" because there will come a time in your life when you will want to move on from the past, however, could be snared by the words spoken prior. You must remember that the pain of past hurts and promises to never let go can put you in bondage, keeping you tied to the past.

What we need is *freedom* from the hurt, unforgiveness, the psychological wounds, the painful memories, the broken heart, and the emotional baggage that interferes with enjoying your life. When Jesus heals those past hurts, He transforms the memories by removing the pain.

I never thought that I'd be on the other side of life encouraging people, especially coming from a place where I was pregnant as a teenager, in a domestic violent relationship, had an abortion, smoking and drinking a lot, didn't know my purpose in life, and so much more shows just how good and merciful God is!

We are created to add value and shine bright in a dark world. It's challenging to be a bright light shining in such a dark world if you are in darkness yourself. If we are living in deep turmoil and pain, how can we offer a helping hand to those who are also in the same position as us? There is a saying that goes "We can't give what we don't have." That is not to say our life must be perfect before we choose to make an impact in our generation, however, we must work towards

The Garden of My Soul

being transformed into the best versions of ourselves because what you do flows from who you are. That person who you always dreamed of becoming can still be. I say this to you:

"ARISE [from the depression and prostration in which circumstances have kept you. Rise to a new life]! Shine (be radiant with the glory of the Lord), for your light has come, and the glory of the Lord has risen upon you!"
Isaiah 60:1 AMPC

I live in the countryside, so when I am driving down country lanes at night, I am petrified. Nonetheless, as soon as I see a little light barely shining from the lamp post, I feel at peace. The light represents hope leading me through the darkness. That's what Jesus did for me. I was in a lot of darkness, but Jesus was the light that showed me the way out but also made me become a light to others.

Before I became born again, my life was in darkness. I was in a position where I knew I would be someone great and influential one day. When I say 'being someone great,' I mean walking in my purpose which was what I felt my soul was crying out for. I did not get the definition of what my soul was longing for until I opened up to Jesus Christ.

The Garden of My Soul

To be totally honest, when reading this book, you will read a lot about how Jesus saved me. This is not because I am trying to push Him down your throat; I just can't tell the story without telling you what He did. He is the main character. I would be lying and trying to put on a façade if I said I have a complete formula to give you on how to get out of your mess (whatever your mess might be). I can only share the lessons learnt on the way. The aim is to share my journey to encourage you that nothing is impossible.

Where you are right now is not a representation of your future. You can refuse to settle for less in life. You can be free; you can be healed and you can become whole. This isn't a book on survival and I pray you will know that you can still thrive.

CHAPTER ONE

The Perfect Garden

Before I delve into the garden of my soul, I want to talk about the first garden that was ever made; the *Garden of Eden* which was a perfect garden. In Genesis 2:15 (Amplified version), the Bible says: *"So the Lord God took the man He had made and settled him in the Garden of Eden to cultivate and keep it."*

God placed man in the garden to maintain it. That is powerful to me because although it was a perfect garden, it still needed to be maintained. Everything God made was perfect until the serpent came in and deceived man making them question their identity. The serpent deceived Eve to believe that if she ate the fruit, she would be like God.

At that point, Adam and Eve's identity was distorted because it made them question what God told them and question who they are. In an instant, they had forgotten they were already made in the image of God.

The Garden of My Soul

Yes, we inherited sin and our souls are like our own private garden. Whatever you allow into your garden, whatever you speak into your garden and whatever you sow into your garden is what will grow in your garden.

Adam and Eve were two humans who were innocent; they were living a life without shame and guilt, until they yielded to the temptation of the serpent. Do you remember when you were a child? You were innocent. We did not ask to be born, however, along the way, things happened to the garden of our souls. We go through things in life that hurt us, scar us and leave us in a state where we feel traumatised.

Unfortunately, the things that happen to us throughout our lives may not be our fault, however, it is still our responsibility to maintain the garden of our souls. It almost feels like a daily battle of striving to get back to a place where we were happy, care-free, healed, set free and walking in our purpose, however, it is possible to get back to that place where we once were; it will just take work.

The Bible says that *God planted a garden* – this shows that in everything, there is a process. For God to plant, there must have been a seed involved. Whatever we want in life doesn't come with a wave of a wand, it comes with a *seed* being planted.

The Garden of My Soul

Anyone that plants a seed has a plan to see it grow, whether negative or positive. When the seed grows, the challenging part is knowing how to maintain what has been planted, or if it is a bad seed, knowing how to uproot it. The lesson here is that either way, it will take work.

As I mentioned above regarding everything being a process, we must understand that we have to go through a process in life. At times we can look at another person's life and see their end result, not knowing the work they had to put into it or aware of the seeds they had to uproot, plant and maintain which gives an illusion to some that if we overlook our mess, it will disappear. Working towards our freedom will require uprooting deep issues that was planted in our childhood growing up including the wrong words that were spoken over our lives by our teachers, our own parents or even ourselves.

I remember at school; my teacher said these exact words to me: "Your life is going to go down the swanee!" The meaning and origin of the phrase *down the swanee* refers to "completely lost or wasted" — synonymous phrases: down the pan – down the toilet – down the tube(s) – down the plughole – down the drain – down the gurgler. Isn't it funny how I still remember these words? WORDS!

Whether negative or positive are seeds which grow, and if the former should never be entertained, make sure you uproot every negative word that was or **is** spoken over your life, for Proverbs 18:21 says that life and death are in the power of the tongue.

Take care of the garden

"The LORD God took the man and put him in the Garden of Eden to work it and take care of it."

Genesis 2:15 (NIV)

Are you tending to the garden of your soul, or do you believe it will take care of itself? God told Adam to look after what He gave him because gardens need to be taken care of. When I was a single mother living in Hackney, I used to look out the window into my neighbour's garden.

It was so beautiful which was understandable, as she was always working on it. There was my garden looking like a pea green colour, but for me, I had no understanding of what to do with the garden.

I've never operated a lawn mower coupled with laziness which resulted to my garden as a complete mess. Similarly, we can't covet what someone else has without being willing to put in the work to attain it. For example, we cannot look at someone else's marriage and assume that it's perfect by chance, not knowing the work that couples put into making their marriage successful.

The Garden of My Soul

You may not see the work married couples do behind the scenes; the seeds they sow and the weeds they pluck up. This also applies to the prosperous ministries you see other people enjoying and attending. You haven't seen the hours of sleep they've had to sacrifice for in prayer and the finances they've given to see the work of God flourish. This also relates to when we see other children behaving well and feeling out of place when your child misbehaves.

In 2019, I remember sharing a part of my story to students during a PSHE (personal, social, health and economic) lesson to encourage them to make the right choices for their futures. One of the students replied "Miss, well you seem fine now; look where you are today!"

My response to the student was "I may be where I am today, but you have no idea of the journey I had to go through to get to this point; you have a chance to get it right now. Why would you want to experience challenges yourself when you have someone standing in front of you that's gone through the process and telling you not to go down that path?"

The point is, you can't enjoy what you haven't cultivated or worked on thoroughly and you cannot look at someone's life assuming they just arrived there.

The Garden of My Soul

We are placed in our own gardens to cultivate it so let's do some practical work below. Allow the Holy Spirit to guide you and lead you to the answers, ask for wisdom:

"The Spirit of the LORD will rest on him. The Spirit of wisdom and of understanding; the Spirit of counsel and of might; the Spirit of the knowledge and fear of the LORD."

Isaiah 11:2 (NIV)

Journal Section:

Write down the negative seeds that were sown or are still being sown in your life. These seeds can represent words spoken over your life, negative attitudes that people have portrayed or what you have done to yourself:

_____
_____
_____
_____
_____
_____
_____
_____
_____
_____
_____

The Garden of My Soul

___

What are the areas in your life that you know need to be worked on?

CHAPTER TWO

My Mess

I've spoken about how gardens can get messy. Now, I want to share my mess with you. The garden of my soul that needed a lot of work. Before I gave my life to Christ, my life was in complete turmoil. As a young girl looking for love at the age of 16, I thought I found it in a boy. There was a void in me that needed to be filled. I had no consistent father figure in my life and was craving for love.

I remember the day I found out that I was pregnant which came as a shock. I was 18 living at home and was not ready for a baby. Thoughts of abortion came to me due to the fear of having to face my mum and family; what would they say? What would they think of me? I was so embarrassed.

At the age of 19, I had my first daughter, and my relationship was very abusive. In the relationship, I continuously asked myself how I had got there. It's important for me to point out that the relationship didn't start off abusive. We were just two young people into each other, but things gradually changed. For me, it started off with verbal abuse in an argument, shouting and using derogatory words, then hearing countless apologies. I also found myself making excuses for him, "Oh, he only said those

The Garden of My Soul

words because he was angry and he has apologised so it's fine!" Then, it happens again and before you know it, he hit me and it soon became the norm. For a long time, I used to believe it was my fault and that I had mental problems.

When my ex and I first met, I never saw any signs of him saying or doing the things he did. He was a gentleman, kind, loving and sweet. Until we had a disagreement. When we argued, I met a different version of him. It was during the arguments we had that his true colours came out. He became snappy, not only to me but to those who were around him too; which was a red flag.

A warning to those who are not yet married and in a relationship – be with your partner long enough to analyse them under pressure. Understand them in their lows as well as their highs. Before jumping into the deep end with that person, observe them in different situations and see how they interact with their family and friends. Speak with their family and friends. I'm sure they have stories to tell.

Looking back, I was warned from the beginning. My mum and family members around me were immediately against our relationship from the beginning as the first time I introduced them to him, he was on tag by the police. When I look back, I ask myself, 'What was I thinking?' I now understand that every teenager is different. Not every teenager did the things I did, however, there are a lot of teenagers who

The Garden of My Soul

feel like they know it all. I was one of those teenagers. I was living in my own mist; my own world despite many warnings.

Abuse, whether verbally or physically was happening on and off for years and up to this day, I can't remember what our arguments were over. <u>What could be so bad that he had to put his hands on me? What did we argue over that the one who was *meant to love me* felt the need to push my head against a brick wall unapologetically?</u> During that time, I thought I knew more than I did. I am so far removed from that teenage girl that I continuously tried to understand how that version of me thought this was okay. I remember one day, he locked me outside of our home. It was so bad that one of the crack-addicts who lived next door came out and took me in their home to comfort me as I cried bitterly. I don't know where that woman is today, but if she reads this book, thank you.

That was one of my lowest moments. In the middle of my tears and anguish, I asked myself: "How did I get here? How did I allow him to do this to me?" I didn't have an answer.

When I finally calmed down, I realised that I, Tara, had allowed myself to get so low, as I was being made safe in a crack house. I remember the lady kindly offering me a cup of tea, but I couldn't accept it. My mind was preoccupied with thoughts; I needed to get out of there. Not out of her house, but out of this horrible situation that had become my life. So, I

The Garden of My Soul

politely rejected the offer for tea with a "No thank you, I am fine now" and a weak smile. Maybe a part of me felt like accepting the tea would be accepting comfort in this situation. I didn't want comfort. I wanted to get out!

With this resolve and revelation in my mind, you'd think that was my turning point, but there I was, again, a couple of days later at his house. After a few *I'm sorry* apologies and *I'll never do it again*, I was back in his arms pretending like nothing happened. I want to make you aware that domestic violence is real, and you need to be wise when you put all your emotions in one person.

You don't want to believe that your partner will ever hurt you again, or you won't feel alone. You may be scared to tell people what you are going through due to embarrassment. I was embarrassed because I was already warned by my family that he was not good for me. I did not want to hear those famous words "I told you so," I wanted to prove them wrong.

I felt that maybe one day, he will change so all I have to do is hold on a little longer. Someone who is experiencing you may be 'holding' on to the belief that one day, he or she will change, it will get better, or even worse; believing that you deserved it. Every time after an incident, I would be told that it was my fault and that if I just did or didn't do a particular thing, he wouldn't have flipped. If you are reading this and you are in a similar relationship, just know that you

The Garden of My Soul

do not deserve it, there is nothing you did to deserve being disrespected. Do not settle for less; you are worth more.

I kept everything to myself as I was embarrassed and ashamed to tell my friends and family members. I was hoping someone would see through me and notice that I needed a helping hand. Although I pushed everyone away and I admit that, I was also desperate for someone to see beyond my brave face. I am not sure the reason why I continually put on a brave face around my friends. Maybe because I was one of the popular girls at school and did not want to mess up my reputation.

It's amazing the stories we tell ourselves about how other people will perceive us, which most of the time we are wrong about. Just know you won't win the battle being silent. Looking back, being in a domestic violent relationship impacted my relationships with family and friends.

I can think of a few incidents, such as when I attended a comedy club with my friends to see Kojo. One of my friends stated that 'my body was there at the show, but I was not there.' It was almost as if my mind was somewhere else. She then continued to explain my phone ringing and me rushing out of the venue to answer the phone to my ex. After finishing with the call, I came back, sat down for a little bit and then rushed back out as I needed to go.

The Garden of My Soul

Another incident which changed the trajectory of my relationship with my friends was when I was at my mum's house with my ex; we were arguing about something, and he pushed over some furniture in my mum's house with so much rage. I remember being slapped and the door knocking. I went to the door to see who it was and as I looked through the keyhole, there were my friends outside in a happy and jolly mood, calling my name from the other side of the door.

It was almost as if they knew I was there. I remember going back into the living room and closing the door. I was aware that they knew I was in; however, I did not want to open the door and have them see me crying and looking like a complete state. Continuous incidents like these impacted my friendships in the long term. Their frustration was that they thought I was choosing a boyfriend over our friendship. I was subconsciously pushing them away and it took many years to fully reconcile with them again.

Not only my friends, but bit by bit, I was also pushing my family away. I remember one day, my mum and sister turned up at my house without notice; deep down I did not mind, but my partner at the time did. I remember him saying to me 'my family were disrespecting me because they just turned up at the house without giving notice and I need to communicate this to them because it is disrespectful.' I don't know what it was at the time that made me believe it straight away.

The Garden of My Soul

There I was, a couple of days later ringing my family telling them they should not come to the house without giving me notice. Certain incidents that took place with my family ruined our relationship in the long-term. One of the many ways it ruined my relationship long-term is that many years after my second child was born, I expected love and support.

I expected my family to randomly knock at the door with smiles, cakes and flowers. Unfortunately, this did not happen, which caused more division between us because now I was offended and confused as to why they were being withdrawn. When I finally pulled them aside to find out what was wrong and why they did not come to see me, that was when I realised the way I treated them when I had my first daughter and was informing them about the way they were treating me.

Once I was able to have some uncomfortable conversations with my family and friends over time, our relationships started to make progress. Our biggest barrier was communication and understanding. Communication is key in every relationship coupled with understanding, as I always wonder how things would be now if we didn't communicate.

My experience with having a child at such a young age, caused me to fall into a state of depression. I always felt sad which caused me to smoke and drink alcohol. I almost felt like I tried to find ways to keep

The Garden of My Soul

myself on a high. I really wanted to be happy and without the large consumption of alcohol or without smoking, I fell right back down into low moods. There was a void in my soul that I wanted to fill. "Why did I stay?" was the question most people asked. Many times, I did want to leave the relationship, but I feared having the reputation of the 'single baby mother' stereotype that would've labelled me. I didn't enjoy being a mother and thought I'd lost my life.

Now I know legally an 18-year-old is seen as an adult, but the truth is I was a child who had a child. I was supposed to enjoy those years of going to university, investing in my future, going on holiday and socialising with my friends, but, there I was, tied down with responsibility.

I remember when my first child was just a few days old and my friends came to visit me. They were all dressed up and ready to go out. The reality of me not being able to go with them whilst having milk leaking from my breasts hit me big time. All I could do from that point was to move forward, although I didn't know how to.

The fear of life and being lonely gripped me. I was a mother of a young child and having to grow up so fast, living with my boyfriend at such a young age, and not having enough money for food or nappies.

The reality for me was having to use one of my period pads as a nappy for one night. Waking up to a crying

The Garden of My Soul

baby everyday with nowhere to go and no money was torture. No matter how much alcohol I'd consumed or drugs I took, the void in my soul was still empty as the sensational feeling I would get from drinking and smoking only lasted for a moment and was replaced by more drinking and drugs.

Earlier in the book, I stated that *'pain forms a type of bondage'* because the more I'd consumed alcohol and drugs, it led to me believing those were the only things that made me happy, but it didn't. It made me dependant on them. This is how many people fall into addictions and can't be dealt with. However, there is someone who knows how to get YOU out of all the mess and His name is **Jesus**.

The moment when life started changing for me was when I gave my life to Christ which was the best decision I made. I got saved on the bus by a sweet old Caucasian lady who ministered to me and led me to the Lord. I remember sitting on the 276 bus in Hackney looking out of the window into the grey sky, plotting and contemplating committing suicide. The lady came and sat next to me and started talking to me about Jesus. She asked if I knew Jesus.

I then realised that I'd heard of Jesus, but did I *really* know Him? Did I read the bible? The answer was *no*, which she then led me to repeat a word of prayer after her, known as the sinner's prayer.

The Garden of My Soul

As I repeated after her, tears started falling down my eyes, and eventually, the lady got up and left the bus. I would love to meet that lady again and thank her for introducing me to the most amazing person ever, Jesus Christ! My life had meaning from that point; did I look the same? Yes! Was my situation the same? Yes! But something happened deep down. I had a hunger for more! I wanted to know more about Jesus.

My childhood friend was going to a church called Salem International Christian Centre, which I was led to ask her for the details. At this point, I was still with my ex and thought that if I could bring him on the same journey of going to church, I would start seeing changes and our relationship would be fixed.

Unfortunately, that was not the case! We must understand that our journey isn't the same as someone else's journey. The decisions we make outside of God has nothing to do with God. When it is not His will, there is nothing we can say or do to make it His will.

Reading the Bible and going to church is a big part of my testimony which I will never leave out. Being consistent in these things helped my confidence as I was not a confident person. I did not know my worth and my value; because of this, I allowed people, situations and circumstances to frame who I was. Eventually, it felt as if scales fell from my eyes and I finally saw how valuable I am, how strong I am, how powerful I am. I was my own biggest barrier to making progress and I could not grow whilst trying to hold on to my old life.

At this point, I felt like I needed to do something; I needed my actions and decisions to reflect my new state of mind. After all, I am better than this. I was ready for my life to change and God was filling me with courage and boldness. So, one day, my ex went out with his friends. In the middle of the night, I suddenly woke up and decided that this was the end. I started to pack his clothes in a suitcase and put them outside the door.

My heart was racing because I didn't know how he would respond to this, what was going to happen next? This was one of the biggest decisions I was going to make. As I was packing his bags, I heard the words he'd spoken replaying in my mind *"No one will want to be with you with a child"* and *"You will ruin our child's life because you are splitting up the family."*

Eventually, I heard him reversing into the driveway. Seeing his suitcase, he jumped out of the car demanding I open the door. I was so scared but didn't want to cause a scene, so I opened the door. As I tried to call the police, his hands reached for my neck, his cold finger wrapped around it, strangling me all the while I tried to call the police. My daughter walked out into the corridor shouting "Mummy!"

The Garden of My Soul

He grabbed my phone as I tried to call the police, but he threw it away, dragging my legs back as I crawled for the phone. Sirens were heard in the distance which he then realised were getting closer as he headed to the front door and drove away. I was left in the house crying with the police at the door taking pictures of the bruises on my neck. This was it – this was the end! I knew I deserved better; I knew that God had a greater plan for me.

"For I know the plans I have for you, declares the Lord; plans to prosper you and not to harm you, plans to give you hope and a future."

Jeremiah 29:11 (NIV)

A couple of days later, he came back to my house pleading for me to take him back, holding on to my ankles and crying. For a split second, I thought about it as the tears and emotions he displayed made it seem he was sincere. I finally had people I could ask for advice, so I asked my Bishop for his opinion regarding me going back to the relationship. My Bishop looked at me and said these few words that changed my life. He said "Baby, no one can change without God." It was as if those words came alive on the inside of me; those were the only words I needed.

There was a peace I felt deep within which I cannot put into words. It gave me enough confidence to take myself away from the abusive relationship and start a new life.

The Garden of My Soul

Breaking up with my ex was a decision I made for myself and my daughter. Inevitably, becoming that stereotype I was trying to avoid and tried to do everything in my power to get out of the situation I put myself into. Looking back, I can see why many people give up as it takes an intentional mind and the courage to move forward. It takes faith and believing in God for a way out, following His voice for direction.

When you are full, you no longer have an appetite for anything else. This was my experience; I had no appetite for my old life and refused to entertain anything less than my worth and being treated like garbage.

"Blessed are those who hunger and thirst for righteousness, for they will be filled."

Matthew 5:6 (NIV)

Being a single mum wasn't easy and having no one around especially at home was quite depressing. Going out and coming back home alone felt strange, it was something I didn't enjoy, I felt lonely. One of the many things I did not enjoy was food shopping. Uber did not exist back then so without a car was hard and I remember a particular day going to Tesco's on the bus with my daughter. She was I think one years old at the time. I didn't want to bring the buggy because of the drama I would face getting on the packed bus and being turned away by the driver to

The Garden of My Soul

wait for another bus. That day it started to rain heavily as we were coming back home on the bus. My daughter was sleeping and because I didn't want to wake her up. I had to strategise how I'd get off the bus and walk home which was about 10 minutes from the bus stop, alongside all the shopping.

Balancing a baby on my shoulder whilst holding the shopping bags in the rain was a miracle! As soon as I got home, I remember bursting out in tears longing for my situation to change as there was a deep cry for help.

As a young single mother, trying to move forward with my life was the challenge. I was still going to church, praying and reading my bible. I really wanted to discover my purpose in life. I wanted to move on and be a better version of myself.

What did a 'better version of myself' look like at the time? The truth is I didn't know exactly what that looked like, however, one thing I knew was that there was more to me than what happened to me.

Even in my mess, I knew deep down I had a greater purpose. I knew there was something to do but couldn't articulate it. I had visions of preaching to people and had great business ideas that still needed to be explored. None of which happened when I was still in the toxic relationship.

The Garden of My Soul

At some Christian events I went to, men and women of God would point me out to tell me there was greatness on my life. My Bishop would point out there was greatness on my life. The most frustrating thing for me was what I was seeing and hearing about my life did not match my reality.

I remember feeling so lonely and behind in life. I was at home during the week looking after a baby whilst my friends were living the university life. It felt like me and my friends were living in completely different worlds. The significant moments where reality sunk in was waking up every morning having nothing to do other than the continuous pattern of watching 'The Jeremy Kyle Show,' 'Bargain Hunt' and 'Loose women.' My friends on the other hand, were living a care-free life (which was what it looked like through my lenses), going out, working and building great lives for their futures at the right time. Whereas, all I was concerned about was cooking, cleaning and working out how to survive.

This is why I have a great passion for young, single women who are trying to rush ahead or want to grow up fast. I always think, what would I say to my younger self? I would say to my younger self to slow down; you have all the time in the world to take on responsibilities. When you get into a relationship, you want to be an asset, not a liability. Start from now!

Invest in your soul, body and spirit. Invest in yourself financially, build your credit score, work on the debt

The Garden of My Soul

you have to pay off. Invest in your spiritual life, get closer to Jesus and know Him more because you can never graduate from knowing the Lord. There are many things to accomplish and achieve as a single lady or man; there is no reason why you should be bored.

Over the years, on the quest to find out what my purpose was, I was involved with a few network marketing businesses and involved myself in different activities to keep me busy. I loved going to the gym. I used to go to the gym with my Godmother Tina, which is a great memory for me. I felt at my best physically and working out helped me mentally also. My Godmother would pay for me to get facials and would spoil me with buying organic foods. God really used her at that time to make me feel good.

One of the decisions I made which I regret was being moved from the bidding list which would have allowed me to receive a council place, instead, I accepted an offer for private accommodation. I must admit, at the time, my sister warned me regarding being moved from the list and accepting private accommodation.

It was a difficult decision to make because at the time I was thinking about my daughter, I did not want her to live in the council properties they were showing me which had barely any light shining through the windows and lots of mould everywhere. Instead, they showed me a house with beautiful cream carpets

The Garden of My Soul

everywhere, a garden, two bedrooms; everything was just brand new.

During the visit, I remember there being other families waiting outside for me to view the property as I was first on the list. After I viewed the property, they asked me those four words, "Do you want it?" I began to nod my head as I imagined the furniture I would place in each room. I made decisions from the place of guilt. I felt as if I had let my daughter down and that my responsibility was to at least provide her a nice place to live. I made decisions that would satisfy her in that moment without thinking of the long-term cost.

The rent for that property was £398 per week and even though I was receiving housing benefit, it was not full housing benefit as I was working and eventually couldn't afford to maintain the home. The rent was an expense I could not afford which resulted in us being evicted, leaving me homeless for a few weeks.

When I was evicted, my partner (who is now my husband) stood in the gap and helped me move. I have experienced many embarrassing moments in my life; this was one of them. I recently met this guy which I genuinely liked and he was helping me to move home. He was there when the bailiffs came to remove my belongings along with the police. To make it even more embarrassing, he called some of his friends to help me move. I thought at that point, 'That's it; he will call me up tomorrow and end the relationship, whilst

The Garden of My Soul

his friends laugh behind my back,' but that wasn't the case. After that, I stayed for a few weeks on his sister's floor who kindly opened her home to me and my daughter.

Again, embarrassment gripped me and did not want to face the shame of going back to my mum's house to hear the words 'I told you so.' Looking back, I know my mum would have taken me in, however, back then, I didn't believe it. On my part, it was pride and wanting to prove everyone wrong that I can make it on my own. I honestly felt like a failure. It was a very challenging season, however, one great aspect about seasons is that they don't last forever.

If you are reading this book and going through a rough season, what you are experiencing at the moment is temporary.

Don't allow the mess you are in to define you. Trust and believe God! He will definitely see you through and take you out of your mess.

"So, we don't look at the troubles we can see now; rather, we fix our gaze on things that cannot be seen. For the things we see now will soon be gone, but the things we cannot see will last forever."

2 Corinthians 4:18 (NLT)

The Garden of My Soul

Journal Section:

What type of mess are you currently in right now that you want to get out of? Be transparent and possible:

CHAPTER THREE

Rodents in the Garden

Rodents aren't attractive in gardens because they damage the fruits, the seeds, the vegetables, the bulbs and the plants. Rodents can expose people and pets to various diseases. I doubt anyone invites rodents into their gardens, but they show up none the less and can destroy what you are trying to grow. But just because you didn't invite them does not mean you don't have to get rid of them.

Have you ever had someone show up in your life that you didn't invite, you probably didn't think they were harmful, tolerated them and then bam, they messed you up? Even when you find yourself in situations that isn't your fault, you still have to deal with the mess that was left behind. You should take time out to reflect on why you keep attracting people who hurt you or allowing the same situations in your life to make you question yourself.

That's what I had to do and I realised it was a case of the value I placed on myself. The value you place on your life will enable you to set healthy boundaries. Over time, I felt like I was growing and becoming more confident. I was happier, however, I did not yet fully see my value and ended up allowing someone else to walk into my life. I'll share a story with you. This particular man on the scene was a Pastor; a man

The Garden of My Soul

of God I met not long after I started attending church. When I came to church, I didn't go looking to find a man. I came to church because I was desperate for a change. This man started off by having friendly conversations with me. His intentions towards me may have been genuine, however, he came at the *wrong time*. I was still broken, didn't know my purpose and needed a touch from God. I was a single parent who still felt lonely and desired love, so I indulged in the attention he gave me.

Even though I wasn't searching, I was still nursing a hole in my heart, longing for true love, so when something came that looked like it but wasn't it, I let it in. The enemy will always offer you counterfeit love and if you are not careful, you may end up accepting it because you don't know the difference between what true love is and what fake love is.

When you haven't accepted God's unconditional love for you, you won't be able to detect a counterfeit. I was already going to church, but I was far from whole and still had a long way to go. I knew God loved me, but I was still working at believing and accepting it. I wasn't used to consistent love; I hadn't trusted God's love yet so when the Pastor who I naively trusted came, I had no guard up and fell into the same habits.

Shopkeepers are trained to look out for security features on a bank note so they can recognise when they are given a counterfeit bank note. In the same way, we need to know true love so that we are able to

The Garden of My Soul

identify counterfeits who come into our lives to avoid the exchanging of ourselves for something that didn't cost them. A real coin/bank note deserves the exchange of something valuable. Does this resonate with some of you? You may be giving wife benefits to someone who is not even claiming you as a girlfriend and visa versa.

To cut the long story short, I saw him a couple of times. The moment I started attending church on Sundays, he'd asked me to join him and go out with a few of the church members. I didn't think for once he had any interest in me at this point because he didn't ask me out on a date.

A couple of months later, he called me and asked if he could stay at my house because he had other people staying in his own home. As someone who recently became a Christian, I didn't see anything wrong with him staying over, especially if he was downstairs whilst I was upstairs. A few church members informed me that him staying over would be inappropriate, but I just thought they were over exaggerating as Christians do, right? Wrong!

As time went on, he ended up staying at my house for longer than he purposed. Eventually, my feelings for him grew because it felt nice to have a man help me out with my daughter, and also had dinner ready when I got back from work. I mean, who wouldn't want that? He helped out around the house. He was kind and polite. If there was anything I said or did that he

The Garden of My Soul

disagreed with, he would sit down with me and talk through it with me. At the time, I liked that about him, as it was something I had not experienced before, as my last relationship was very hostile. The question I'd always ask myself was *"Am I attracted to him or the acts?"* Or was he filling my void of loneliness?

Maybe, it was that little girl who was crying out for a father-figure. I knew that I wasn't healed or whole yet, but I started developing feelings for him because at that point, we were acting like a couple *without* the title. He went from someone who invited me out with a group, to inviting me out on his birthday; just the two of us. This was where it became confusing as he did not make his intentions known at all. When I would ask him what we are, he would be vague and talk about how I still had a lot of growing up to do. It made me feel like I was not good enough, but he still stayed. I guess this is what people now call a *situationship.*

Whenever we'd go to church together, he would tell me to walk on and that he would meet me inside. The first time he said this, I didn't think anything of it, however, the third and fourth time, I started to question it which was another red flag I chose to ignore and didn't recognise the signs on time.

We eventually slept together, and I became pregnant again! I felt like if he accepted the baby, it would have been ok. It was different this time because though we were not official, I had seen him be caring towards

The Garden of My Soul

me, my daughter and provide a certain level of stability. However, when I told him about the pregnancy, the man who wasn't sure about where we stood and had been stringing me along was finally all of a sudden clear. He knew where he stood with me: what a coincidence! He stated that we couldn't be together, he was disappointed in me and decided to leave the house.

There I was, pregnant again; not married. Left alone again with another man exiting my life. The embarrassment, the shock, the strong feelings of rejection again, consumed me! What a failure I thought I was. The wound ripped open; how will I explain this again? Will anyone understand? How will I cope alone with two children? I felt like I had to make the decision to get rid of the pregnancy.

I spoke to my Bishop and one of my sisters at church because I just couldn't go through in silence. They didn't condemn me. They told me they would help me with the children and that I wasn't alone. While I heard them and appreciated what they said, I just couldn't face the thought of the double stereotype of being a single mum with children from different fathers. I didn't want that to be me. So, I went ahead with the abortion.

To be honest, I didn't know how to feel. I thought I was fine and would just move on, but the truth is, I was numb. If I thought I was broken before, I was wrong. The abortion brought me to a whole new low.

The Garden of My Soul

Maybe because it was the first time something like this had happened while I was a Christian. Maybe it was because I didn't get rid of only one of my children, but two. I was pregnant with twins. I don't know, I was just numb!

What I think was crazy was I think I was more broken about the fact he walked away from me, not about the abortion. But then, I read a book, 'Heaven Is so real' by Choo Thomas. In the book, Choo describes an encounter with Jesus that took her to heaven. There was a part in the book where God showed her a nursery full of children that had been aborted by their parents.

God told her He was looking after them until the mothers who aborted their babies came back to heaven. That caused a flood of tears to come out of me. Jesus had my twins. He was doing what I didn't think I could. I remember thinking about just how kind Jesus was. To be honest, I didn't know I cared that much until I read that book. Prior to that, I was just numb, but reading that part touched a deep place that I had been disconnected with.

With the help of God and my Bishop, I made the decision to heal from it, even though all I wanted to do was crawl under a rock, but I could not give up at that point, even though I wanted to.

This was a turning point for me, at least one of many. I made the decision to stop messing around and the

The Garden of My Soul

boundaries in my life had to be set in order to see God's best.

Whenever I share this story, some people are shocked that I did not leave my church or the Church as a whole. Firstly, it depends on how you perceive your issues. I see the church as a hospital where sick people go. There are many hospitals out there who have a bad reputation for getting things wrong.

Maybe one of the doctors made an error which may have resulted in a patient becoming more sick, or even to the point of death. The hospital will respond by getting rid of that nurse or doctor who made the error. Once that person is removed, it does not mean you would necessarily stop going to that hospital altogether.

Just to clarify, the Pastor I spoke about was not the main Pastor in the church. Thankfully, when I told my main Pastor about it, he was swift to take action and I was satisfied by how the leaders dealt with the situation.

So, what does this have to do with rodents? Research states that rodents seek to find areas to hide under rubbish, timber, wood, drainpipes and sheds to create havoc. When we haven't cleared the rubbish in our gardens (souls), the enemy will find a place to hide. In my case, it was under the loneliness in my soul. I wasn't able to detect that I still was suffering from

The Garden of My Soul

loneliness and brokenness, even though I was now a Christian, so rodents hid and disguised themselves.

Just because you are a Christian, does not mean you don't have work to do in your soul. You have gone through things that have impacted your soul, so to make healthier choices you need to clear the junk in your mind and your emotions so you can live healthier. Many people think that when you become born again, your life changes immediately, not realising that it's a step-by-step process of the journey.

Many people would assume that everything you felt regarding past hurts and pain will just dissolve. Well, I am here to tell you that it won't change without using the correct tools.

We are made up of three attributes:

1) The Spirit
2) The Soul
3) The Body

When you become born again, your spirit becomes born again, not your soul; your soul is made up of your mind, will and emotions. This is why in Romans 12:2 it says that we should not be *conformed to this world but should be transformed by the renewing of our minds, so that you may prove what is the good and perfect will of God, even the thing which is good and acceptable and perfect."*

The Garden of My Soul

You cannot renew something that was not previously there. For example, when renewing your weekly oyster card, you replace the money that's already there. Remember I discussed our original state at the beginning of this book in the perfect garden (our minds were perfect) and the fall of man? This is why we need to 'renew our minds' with His Word.

Along the way in life, there will be several interruptions; the enemy continues to sow his weeds in our souls; we can see this in Matthew 13:25-26 that: *"While he was sleeping, his enemy came and sowed weeds among the wheat and went on his way. So, when the plants sprouted and formed grain, the weeds appeared also."*

We have to be aware of what is growing in our lives, we must identify where certain issues we experience come from. If we don't, we will wake up one day and have no clue how it got there.

Different scenarios can happen to us when we neglect and avoid the spiritual fight that constantly comes into our lives, pretending to move on without taking account of the wounds that our souls are longing for to be healed. Sometimes, we get comfortable in our lives where the plants have sprouted and formed grain, but, for the weeds of the past, they gradually start appearing and choke the good plants that have been placed in our lives.

The Garden of My Soul

This nearly was my experience even in marriage; I was subconsciously angry with the person who was with me based on the person that left. The wounds of my past tried to prevent me from loving new people or embracing new relationships which were my weeds that tried to choke the good things that were growing in my life.

When my husband first approached me, I was scared to love him back. I subconsciously invested 30% of myself but expected 100% back in return. I wasn't fully invested, neither was I giving the best me.

This is the result of the weeds of our past in our lives; it makes you invest only a part of ourselves (30%), and the rest (70%) is tied to a man, woman, dad, mum or whoever hurt you because you haven't fully healed and let go.

The new person coming into your life has no idea that you've been through all that mess. God sends that person into your life, and you've already got a defence set up. Due to this, you chase your blessing away and then eventually end up playing the blame game: "God why did YOU allow this to happen!?" – but God is saying "I have given YOU authority!"

Someone may have sinned against you, or you may have sinned against yourself; all the emotions you've been holding onto is down to you and how you deal with them is by forgiving them and letting them go. If you don't tidy your garden, who will? In this case, it's

The Garden of My Soul

not as simple as paying for a gardener to clean the mess for you.

Similarly, it's not down to your Pastor to do the work for you. This is between you and God to deal with. The question is, *how much do you want to be free?* This is not the work for the lazy; you have to be real before God and talk with the Holy Spirit. God has given us tools which are birthed from the Word of God. We all have been given access to the Word of God which the Holy Spirit will personalise for you to use for your life.

The Bible says in Proverbs 4:23 – "Keep and guard your heart with all diligence, for out of it flows the issues of life." Whatever a person is feeling, it's more than likely they will express it through their speech or will show through their body language or facial expressions. This is why the Bible says in Luke 6:45 (NIV) that "The mouth speaks what the heart is full of."

If a person is feeling depressed or angry, they will most likely speak out of their anger against themselves or others which can put the individual in a deeper hole. Whatever we say, good or bad words are *very powerful*. The same way God told Adam in Genesis 2:15 to keep the Garden neat, tidy and clean is the same way God tells us in Proverbs 4:23 to guard our hearts. This is why we need to clean up our gardens.

The Garden of My Soul

Do you remember the perfect garden I told you about earlier? The garden of *Eden. Eden* means *pleasure.*

Genesis 2:10 expresses a river flowing from Eden went out to water the garden. And "From there, the garden was divided and became four river heads. The first is named *Pishon*; it is the one flowing around the whole land of Havilah where there is gold."

You have to be careful what flows into your soul, your heart because what comes into you can either water you to cause you to flourish or can come to drown you. You were created by God with great potential so it means whatever you allow in, will either help you grow from being a potential to realising it or can drown you out.

Look at what happened, the water flowed into the garden then it multiplied and became four riverheads. There is a resemblance; the garden was divided into four river heads just like our hearts are consisting of four chambers.

In John 7:37-38 it tells us that if we are thirsty, we can drink from Jesus and out of our bellies shall flow rivers of living water. That means when the Spirit of God comes into your life and is the One that's watering your soul, you can't but produce life!

That's why you have to guard your heart, be mindful of what flows into it because it can frame your thoughts. Whatever thoughts you have will eventually

The Garden of My Soul

flow out from your heart and become the life you live. One of the riverheads that flowed from the garden went to a land where there is gold. This shows us that if what comes into you impacts you for good, you can make healthier choices and end up in great places and can expand your reach.

If I was careful of what I allowed into my garden (soul), I would have made healthier choices. As the Bible expresses in Proverbs 4:23 that we should guard our hearts with all diligence because out of our hearts flows the issues of life. I can easily write this book and blame everyone, but the truth is, I had a responsibility to guard my heart.

We need to make sure our hearts are connected to the Presence of God. If our hearts are connected to the Presence of God, our hearts will be filled with the good and priceless things of life including peace, joy, love etc.

Once our hearts are in the state where God desires for it to be, that's when we can have true prosperity. Your ability is to prosper in life is connected to the prosperity of your soul. 3 John 2 says "I wish above all things that you prosper and be of good health even as your soul prospers."

If you don't keep careful watch over your garden (your soul), the enemy will plant weeds and destroy

The Garden of My Soul

it, but thank God for garden-tools including prayer, stillness, faith, praise and worship.

If you don't do the work to clear your garden, you give rodents a place to hide. One thing about rodents is that they don't want to be seen, that's why they scurry when you come near to find a place to hide. You have to be mindful of people who come into your life in secret and those who want to have secret relationships with you without being accountable.

Be careful and discerning; those people may not have good intentions to build genuine friendships with you and can easily take advantage of you. Some people are so broken themselves that their brokenness can exploit your own brokenness. I can't say everyone that is like that will have bad intentions, but you can only give what you have and from where you are. Just because it's not intentional does not mean it's ok. Let's be real though, some people don't have good intentions towards you and just come to exploit your vulnerabilities by bringing the counterfeit of what you desire.

A counterfeit is defined as something that's made to look like the original, usually for dishonest and illegal purposes. The enemy will bring counterfeits into our lives who look like the original, however, our response should be to hold them up in the light.

The same as the shopkeeper holding a £10.00 note in the light to be able to detect whether it's a counterfeit,

The Garden of My Soul

we should take responsibility to bring people before God by praying and looking at their actions through the Word of God.

With regards to romantic relationships, one way of safeguarding yourself is by involving your partner. See if they want to meet your family, friends or Pastor.

If they say not yet or that it's too soon, watch how long they will hide away for. I believe the person who is interested in you will not waste your time; they will not string you along but will make their intentions known.

The Garden of My Soul

Journal section:

Write down what you're allowing from the past to have a negative impact on your future. For example, if you are the person that pushes people away due to fear and rejection, express it. Sometimes, we have to put our issues down on paper in order to see them from a bird's eye view so we can deal with them head on. It's either now or never! You must reject them first before they reject you! So, begin to pour out your heart before God:

_____
_____
_____
_____
_____
_____
_____
_____
_____
_____
_____
_____
_____
_____

The Garden of My Soul

Journal section:

Write what you are going through that you feel is too hard to handle – be transparent as possible:

The Garden of My Soul

Then Jesus said, "Come to me all who are weary and carry heavy burdens and I will give you rest. Take my yoke upon you. Let me teach you because I am humble and gentle at heart and you will find rest for your souls. For my yoke is easy to bear, and the burden I give you is light."

*** Matthew 11:28 (NLT)***

"Give your burdens to the LORD, and He will take care of you. He will not permit the godly to slip and fall."

Psalm 55:22 (NLT)

Tip: Speak out what you wrote above and give those burdens to the Lord. Envision yourself picking them up and laying all your troubles at His feet.

CHAPTER FOUR

The Mess

There are physical gardens that look very attractive; gardens that would make most people want to come from their house for a barbeque; the kids wanting to play outside and the birds chirping away. On the other hand, who wants to enjoy their summer in a garden where the weeds have overgrown, the grass withering away and looking like a pea green colour?! Where nothing is in order.

Genesis 2:15 says that *"The Lord God took man and put him in the garden of Eden to cultivate and keep it."* The word *keep* in this context is another word relating to *maintain*.

God placed Adam in a perfect garden and his job was to maintain it. Every garden needs to be maintained despite its imperfections. Even if a garden is perfect, it still needs to be maintained because seasons change and situations occur along the way. Cats jump over fences into gardens and urinate on the plants and research shows that urine burns the roots of the plants.

My question to you is: "What is burning the root of your soul and stopping you from bearing fruit?" You may be thinking you have sowed good seeds in your soul and that you are growing well which is great. However, plants can become weak during difficult

The Garden of My Soul

seasons and rubbish being swept over by the wind in your garden. Challenges and difficulties are a part of life which can weaken us even though we were previously healthy. Have you ever heard someone you thought had it all together say they are tired because of a difficulty they are facing? The enemy does not want you to have a healthy garden (soul) and will always try to find a place to come and ruin your garden; those lovely flowers you've worked hard to grow.

Children who play with the ball throw it over fences whilst weeds growing continually. Seasons can contribute to the beauty or destruction of our gardens. The winter season feels a lot longer and everything feels dark, dingy and wet. During that period, some people suffer from the seasonal affective disorder (aka sad). They feel less happy, more depressed which has been linked to reduced exposure to sunlight.

When I became a single mother, it felt like I was in the winter season. My days felt repetitive and daunting. Because winter is very dark, I felt so lonely. Going to work and picking my daughter from nursery was a consistent routine. Going home to watch the same TV programme with my daughter was the norm. I was the parent who knew all the words and could sing the nursery rhyme songs. Going to bed and waking up to a day that looked the same as yesterday was depressing.

The Garden of My Soul

However, if you look beyond the harshness of the cold winter, there is beauty. I read that "the cold chill of the winter helps seeds awaken and is also needed to control pests and diseases in the garden."- *Gareth Austin*. During my winter season was when I found Jesus; it's when the seed of greatness was awakened in my life. As much as I wouldn't want anyone to go through what I went through and don't wish to go back there, it dawned on me that the winter season was good for the garden of my soul.

It was the harsh winter season that made me realise I needed to be saved and that doing 'life' on my own was not possible. It's funny sometimes when we say that we've found Jesus, I get it, but the truth is, Jesus is the one that finds us. We just respond to His call. Sometimes it just takes that winter season to respond to His call.

At this point, I was finally accessible to be found. The same way He called out to Adam in the garden after he sinned; "Where are you?" is the same way He calls out to us all the time but we hide from Him wrapped in sin and shame thinking we aren't good enough and the truth is we aren't but He loves us anyway and wants us anyway.

In some seasons, our gardens will experience storms. When the storm comes, it will test the root of the plant or tree. This is why we have to be careful what we are feeding our roots with because it is the roots that

The Garden of My Soul

determine the health of the tree. If our roots are not strong enough, it can't survive through the storm.

Matthew 7:24-29 (NIV) says *"Therefore, everyone who hears these words of mine and puts them into practice is like a wise man who built his house on the rock. The rain came down, the streams rose, and the winds blew and beat against that house; yet it did not fall, because it had its foundation on the rock. But everyone who hears these words of mine and does not put them into practice is like a foolish man who built his house on sand. The rain came down, the streams rose, and the winds blew and beat against that house, and it fell with a great crash."*

Autumn and winter are usually when most people stay indoors because the cold is sharp. No one wants to come out which is usually a time of reflection and solitude. As mentioned above, I met the Lord in the winter season and got closer to Him each day which helped me in our relationship. My prayer life grew stronger as I continued praying like never before.

It got to the point where instead of living every day in despair, I felt happier. The Lord gave me the garment of praise for the spirit of heaviness and the oil of joy for mourning in reference to Isaiah 61:3. I would play my favourite worship songs and dance in the kitchen whilst cooking. I started to enjoy my own company as the Lord was causing me to be free which was a process.

The Garden of My Soul

According to research, autumn leaves fall off trees and a leaf's role is being able to turn sunlight into food. To do this, the leaf needs water which comes from the soil and is sucked up through pipes in the trunk and branches leading to the leaves – this can be a very long process for tall trees. If there isn't enough water, the leaf won't look healthy.

The tree doesn't want to waste the good nutrients in the leaf, so it takes it from the leaf back into the stems and roots. This way, they can be recycled. When the leaf is empty, the tree stops holding onto it and falls to the ground blowing them away in a gust of wind.

My autumn season was where the Lord stripped me from all distractions. Over time, as I continued with the Lord, my taste for worldly pleasures (the desire to go raving to numb the loneliness, entertaining guys that I knew were no good for me) as well as the shame and guilt were no longer there. The Lord stripped me from people who were no longer good for my well-being. Just like a tree, you have to learn how to get rid of anything that's stopping you from being the real you and bearing fruit.

You may be in a relationship that isn't from God. You know deep down that relationship is no good, but you continue holding onto it. Instead of the relationship enabling you to flourish, it's draining the nutrition from you. Learn to be like the tree and let that man leave (like the tree lets the leaves be) to put it plainly; let it go.

The Garden of My Soul

Is there anything you are doing that isn't adding value to your life but harbouring negative energy, time, finances, and peace? If the answer is yes, what are you waiting for? Be like the tree and let go! Seasons are temporary which is why it's important to make the most of out of them and learn from what they are endeavouring to teach you. What you don't learn in one season can either elongate that season or affect the next one.

In every season there are tools that can help us get the best out of the garden. There are garden tools we use for various activities which ultimately make our gardens look pleasant. The problem we have is being too lazy to use them or not taking the time to read the manual to understand how they work.

God has given us tools including the Word of God alongside destiny helpers that He sends to be part of our journey. We have many tools in the 21st century and the churches where we are planted in. We have Pastors, sermons on YouTube, various social media platforms; we have so much to learn from them, however, if you hear the word of God or the godly advice given but don't put them into practice, your foundation will be unstable.

The different seasons I encountered in the past played a big part of my messy garden, however, they birthed in me the seed of humility because I know if it wasn't for God, I wouldn't be where I am today. I won't boast in what I have or who I've become as if I am self-

The Garden of My Soul

made. I am who I am by the grace of God. My seasons birthed seeds of persistence and resilience. I no longer wanted to just speak about surviving. That was good but in my new-found freedom in God, I knew there was more to life than just surviving, I can now thrive. Prior to having my first daughter I was in college but failed and did not even think I could get to higher education. However, once I gave my life to Christ, I started dreaming bigger. First was my desire to go into higher education to further my academics.

Finally, my insides, my soul and my outsides were aligning. What is shown on the outside is a state of what's going on internally.

Proverbs 15:13 (NIV) says that *"A happy heart makes the face cheerful, but heartache crushes the spirit."*

There was a time in my walk with God where I was fed up with looking as if I was free, but not *actually* being free. I was faking it, hoping to make it. I looked happy to others, but, when I arrived home, there was inner turmoil and unease deep in my soul. Those issues were dormant waiting to be triggered, and when they were triggered, there it was! My past sprouted up like the weeds in the garden.

If we are bitter, it can affect our relationships in the future. When I was single, I never thought I had much work to do regarding my character until I got married. When I was single, there was no one around to point

The Garden of My Soul

out my thought patterns. I understand that this isn't a relationship book, but I do want to give this word of encouragement: when you are single and is living with your parents, friends or housemates, use it as an opportunity to be attentive to the negative traits or thought patterns people point out about you. Don't just ignore them and think people are just 'hating' on you. They could be but first take the time to reflect. Especially if its multiple people that don't know each other and people that you know love you.

Work on those weaknesses with the help of the Holy Spirit before getting into marriage. Am I saying you have to be perfect? No, of course not, but the more you work on yourself, the better it will be for your spiritual and mental well-being.

God has His way of guiding His children towards the right path and all you have to do is place your faith and trust in Him. I give the analogy when speaking at events that no one is able to see the spot on their own face until they either look in a mirror or have someone else point it out. That is how it is in marriage.

When we get closer to each other, we begin to see each other's spots, flaws and weaknesses which a vulnerable place to be. You have to learn how to die to self in marriage. It's the same when we get closer to the Word of God. Through His Word, we see our state, sins and flaws, but thank God for Jesus who shed His Blood for us. He is not showing us our flaws

The Garden of My Soul

to condemn us but to help us see where we need to repent and realign.

Please note that just because the work Christ did on the Cross is finished doesn't mean there isn't further work to do. Yes, in Christ we are made perfect, and we are clean. However, there is still work to do in our minds which is a part of our soul. The process of renewing our mindset is where our effort comes in. The wounds of the soul can affect our mind, our will and our emotions which cause us to harbour wrong thoughts. This is dangerous as once a negative thought comes to mind; you must capture it before it penetrates in your heart.

"We demolish arguments and every pretension that sets itself up against the knowledge of God, and we take captive every thought to make it obedient to Christ."

2 Corinthians 10:5 (NIV)

When we become born again, our spirit is made instantly perfect so problems we face in life doesn't come from our spirits but our souls. Our souls aren't born again which is why the Bible says in Romans 12:2 (NLT): *"Don't copy the behaviour and customs of this world, but let God transform you into a new person by changing the way you think. Then you will learn to know God's will for you which is good and pleasing and perfect."*

The Garden of My Soul

It's our souls that needs renewal as well as our mind, will and emotions because they've been wounded by sin and trauma. The problem with most of us is that we don't want to do the work that's needed to transform us into a new person. When you change the way you think, you'll be able to see, understand and do the Will of God for your life and work towards the woman or man God destined for you to be.

Journal Section:

A) Write down your thought patterns that needs to be renewed in your life – be as transparent as possible:

_____
_____
_____
_____
_____
_____
_____
_____
_____
_____
_____
_____

The Garden of My Soul

B) How has your thoughts affected your life? - be as transparent as possible:

The Garden of My Soul

_____
_____
_____
_____
_____
_____
_____
_____
_____

C) Write down <u>two</u> negative thoughts your mind constantly consumes. If there is not enough space below, you can continue on another sheet of paper. Find a promise for each one and for five minutes, focus your mind on it. For example, if you are worried about a particular sickness or pain in your body, find a Bible scripture that reflects healing and meditate on it. If you are worried about your future, find some promises of God about your future and meditate on it (you can google it). Speak the scripture back into your situation:

Negative thought 1:

_____
_____
_____
_____

The Garden of My Soul

God's promise to me:

The Garden of My Soul

Negative thought 2:

The Garden of My Soul

God's promise to me:

The Garden of My Soul

_____
_____
_____
_____
_____
_____
_____
_____
_____
_____

Just like the tree explained above, make a list of who and what do you need to let go of?

_____
_____
_____
_____
_____
_____
_____
_____
_____
_____

The Garden of My Soul

Additional notes page:

The Garden of My Soul

CHAPTER FIVE

The Turnaround

Let me bring you into another turn around moment for me. During my single season when I lived in Hackney, the garden was clean, and I enjoyed being in it with my first daughter having a good time and relaxing. Over the years, whilst I was there, I hadn't paid much attention to the garden. During my years of living in Hackney, the lawn got mowed once by one of the Pastors from my church.

After that one time, the grass began to grow again, and the weeds became taller; the grass looked like a moulded pea green colour. My daughter couldn't play out in the garden, and I couldn't hang my washing on the line. The garden wasn't being used to its fullness of what it was made for. Isn't that the same with us? When we allow the garden of our souls to wither, we won't be used by God effectively to the fullness of what we were made for.

One day, when I was off from work, I sat on a chair in my living room when I heard the Lord tell me to get up. I knew it was the Spirit of God speaking as there was a strong echo in my spirit. The Lord said I should look at my garden. I went to the window and looked out of the garden. Then, the Lord said to me "How your garden looks is how you look within."

The Garden of My Soul

I was so amazed at hearing this because I definitely knew it was God because I would not say that to myself! God started to instruct me step-by-step on how to work on my character by using the garden as an illustration. When you read the Bible, God loves to use plants, gardens and trees to illustrate, but this time, the Lord blessed me with my own personal revelation.

One week from that day, I called my neighbour to help me with the garden. As she looked into the garden, she was shocked and stated that a lot of work had to be done. So, the Lord took me back and reminded me of the advice the neighbour gave on how to tidy the garden. The advice she gave was to pluck out all the weeds. Then the Lord spoke to me again and said, "The weeds represent past hurts." Even though I had grown in God, the weeds were affecting the plants from the good seeds that had been sown.

My neighbour advised me to use a weed killer spray. According to research, chemical weedkillers take the hard work out of weeding and is very efficient in getting rid of weeds from the root. The Lord told me that I have to continually use the Word of God to make sure the weeds don't appear again. For us to be able to embrace our futures, we have to assess our past to know what to pluck up. Jeremiah 31:28 says: "Just as I watched over them to uproot and tear down and to overthrow, destroy and bring disaster, so I will watch over them to build and to plant declares the Lord."

The Garden of My Soul

Whatever you uproot will need to be replaced with the right seed. Uproot the negative thoughts and replace them with right-thinking. Replacing a word or thought takes work.

You can't enjoy what you don't cultivate. For some, the issue isn't the planting, or even the building; the issue is the cultivating. Cultivating takes a lot of effort to develop and improve a specific area in our lives which is where most people give up. Even though you mow the lawn and make it clean, it doesn't mean you should give away your garden tools. You will need them again to cultivate it. Similarly, even though God turned my life around, I still faced trials and tribulations. My garden tools are constantly needed to maintain what the Lord has for me.

The motivation to be consistent in my walk with God came from the understanding that I can only cultivate something I value knowing that eventually, I will reap the rewards later.

I had to clean my life up with the help of the Holy Spirit so that I could have a successful relationship with my future. I remember an event in my church for couples. We went to a place called 'Kew Gardens' which is the world's leading botanic gardens. We discovered the maintenance that was needed to keep the garden beautiful. It's an everyday work that's

The Garden of My Soul

needed to keep the garden intact where people can enjoy. Are you willing to pay the price to maintain the garden of your soul? Are people able to enjoy your company because of how beautiful you've become, not just on the outside, but also on the inside? We love to spend time in gardens that are aesthetically pleasing.

God showed me the grass that had been cut in my garden from one the Pastors who helped me previously. Due to laziness, I would brush the old grass to the corner of the garden but doing this made the new weeds grow and covered the old grass. The Lord showed me this because as time passes, it doesn't mean the hurt from the past will heal immediately, neither is it okay to cover up pain and assume it will go away.

The statement 'Time is a healer' isn't true. Time is not a healer; time is a revealer. If you don't deal with your past hurts, it will remain in your heart just like the grass and weeds.

I didn't bother to remove the debris but allowed the new weed to grow over it. I might not have seen it, but it was still there. I used my time to pray a lot! I prayed to God asking Him to heal me because the pain kept sprouting up in other situations. I also spent a lot of time studying the Word and meditating on it. The Word really helped me replace wrong mindsets and see myself the way God sees me. I uprooted toxic

The Garden of My Soul

things in prayer and planted the seed of the word in my heart so I can see godly things grow. It wasn't overnight but I was committed to the process.
This is why God gave us His Word as the right tool.

I also engaged at church especially when the word was preached. I was hungry! I listened to the Word at church, bought the CDs of my Bishop's teachings and played them back over and over again, I listened to sermons on God Channel like 'Enjoying Everyday Life' by Joyce Meyer, Dr Myles Munroe, TD Jakes, Pastor Benny Hinn, Dr Yonggi Cho, Derek Prince, etc and took a lot of notes and went over them when alone. For me, since the word of God brings light and life, I wanted it all.

Sometimes we think hearing the word once is enough. How many times have we heard Pastors preach but never meditate on what was spoken after it was preached? Do you go over the notes during Sunday service and check the scriptures yourself? How many times should we go to church conferences or worship nights and not act on the Word we hear? The Bible says in James 1:22 (NIV) that we should not merely listen to the Word and so deceive yourselves but to do what it says!

Hearing a praise and worship song doesn't make you a Christian but taking action and being obedient to God behind closed doors. I made it a point to go beyond listening to obeying and acting on what the word said. To some I was extreme, but they hadn't

The Garden of My Soul

been where I had been, they heard parts of my story but did not know the desperation for God it birthed in me. I imagine I was like a dry ground that would absorb any water you poured on it. Even though I was not comparing myself to others, I felt like I had lot years and was behind schedule, so I wanted to get all God had for me. The devil had stolen and cheated me enough. I was not going to let anyone shame me into thinking I was doing too much.

Getting my garden back to its flourishing state also required the turning of the soil. This represented turning away from sin. Let me tell you, just because you are committed to God does not mean you will not be tempted to sin. Even though I was determined to not make the same mistakes, temptations were still coming my way. I was not perfect, but I was seeing signs of wholeness because I was making better choices, saying no to what I knew was not of God. I chose to turn away from sin to keep my soul healthy.

Journal Section:

1. Write all the weeds you need to uproot in your life. Read chapter 6 again for a deeper understanding and guidance using Galatians 5:19:

_____

_____

_____

The Garden of My Soul

_____

2. Ask the Holy Spirit for specific scriptures to spray on those weeds that are distracting you. Remember that you don't want the weeds to grow back. Write down the steps you'll take to spend time with the Lord and commit to them:

_____

The Garden of My Soul

Additional notes/key scripture:

The Garden of My Soul

_____

3. Anything you uproot at this present moment in time needs to be replaced with a *good* seed. Begin to prophecy using the word of God. For example, one of the scriptures I spoke over my life was Isaiah 61:3 which reads: *"To appoint unto them that mourn in Zion, to give unto them beauty for ashes, the oil of joy for mourning, the garment of*

The Garden of My Soul

praise for the spirit of heaviness, that they might be called trees of righteousness, the planting of the Lord, that He might be glorified."

The revelation I gained from Isaiah 61:3 is that God is replacing my mourning with joy; my heaviness with praise, and will give me a reason to praise Him, and will be a beautiful plant that will bring glory to God. The Lord will make your life beautiful so that people will want to know Jesus. Now, what's yours? Be specific as you write:

_____
_____
_____
_____
_____
_____
_____
_____
_____
_____
_____
_____
_____
_____
_____

CHAPTER SIX

The Make Up

The same way women apply make-up to enhance their beauty is the same way we need to continually use the Word of God to make us beautiful internally and externally. Whatever is on the inside will eventually show on the outside making our close friends, partner, husband, wife, and family members want to be around us and enjoy our company. God wants our gardens to be like what He previously made in Eden; that is why Jesus came – to connect us back to our original state with the Father. We are made perfect through His son, Jesus Christ.

In Mark 4:31, Jesus explains that *"The Kingdom of God being like a grain of mustard seed when sown into the ground is the smallest of all seeds upon the earth, yet after it is sown, it grows up and becomes the greatest of all garden herbs and puts out large branches so that the birds of the air are able to make nests and dwell in its shade."*

The revelation I received when reading Mark 4:31 is don't despise the size of the godly seeds you're sowing in your life. That seed will grow and become a great and healthy tree. Sometimes we can measure things wrongly and think they will make no impact but trust me. Who I am today is not who I was when I first started by journey in God. What looked like a

The Garden of My Soul

small time of prayer or bible study has contributed greatly to who I am today. Don't give up on sowing good seeds in your life because one day, your small seed will sprout up and become so big that you won't be able to control the growth! Your tree will increase so that you'll be able to provide for others. You'll be an asset to those around you and people who are in need.

This chapter is called 'the make up' because God has beautified my life in many ways. Joyce Meyer in some of her sermons would say this statement: "I may not be where I want to be but thank God I am not where I used to be!" My life isn't perfect; however, God has changed my situation around, and it started from the first day I gave my life to Christ on a bus in Hackney. Ever since then, everything I've done has been by faith.

I didn't have big faith as such, but you don't need big faith to start doing great things. Jesus said:

"If you have faith the size of a mustard seed, you can say to this mountain, 'move from here to there' and it will move. Nothing will be impossible for you."

Mathew 17:20

For example, when I wanted to go back to university as a single mother. I was working at Selfridges at the time and got to the point where I knew that was not where I was supposed to be. I longed to be in my

The Garden of My Soul

purpose. The pull to go back to school was strong and I heard the Lord tell me to leave Selfridges. Realistically, leaving didn't make sense as I had no other way to make money, rent was £398.00 a week, still needed to buy food and everything else my daughter needed, and university was also not free though I knew I could get student loan. I sought for help from the Council to see if there was anything they could do to help me through the transition but was turned down many times as they continued to state the fact that I'd have to pay full rent if I wanted to attend university.

There was so much going on at the same time, there was a stronger desire to change my life, to give myself a chance even though my financial situation was telling me it was impossible.

Everything seemed to happen simultaneously as this was around the time my partner proposed to me. My fiancé (now husband) had previously asked that I leave Selfridges, but I didn't know how to just let it go Selfridges was my safety net. However, when God spoke directly to me about leaving, I knew it would be ok,

When I left Selfridges, all my work colleagues were confused as they knew about my situation. They knew I was a single mother who was barely making ends meet and they expressed this to me telling me I was making the worst decision of my life. When I applied for university, I wasn't aware of the criteria they

The Garden of My Soul

required. I had to pass my GCSE's which wasn't something I achieved in Maths and had to sign up to an adult college course to complete a numeracy diploma to be accepted. Moving forward, I finally left Selfridges and started university.

On the day of my enrolment, the bailiffs came to my house and evicted me and my child as I was in arrears. I had to stay with my now sister in-law's living room floor for some time with which was very degrading, however, I had to keep moving; I couldn't stop now.

At that time, I felt exhausted and embarrassed, feeling like I failed my daughter. The voice of the enemy kept whispering that I made a mistake, and my faith-walk was a load of nonsense. In the midst of it all, the Holy Spirit was cheering me on. He was telling me to keep going and to trust in Him because "Those who put their trust in God shall never be put to shame" – Romans 10:11.

My fiancé at the time managed to find a place for me to rent where it was manageable, and so, my journey began. My journey of starting the life I always wanted – to feel secure and stable. I didn't have all the answers and still don't. My job was just to keep me going whilst trusting God. I am a person who doesn't like sudden changes all at once so while I was grateful things were finally working out, I was rattled.

It felt like I was in a dream, I didn't have a full picture, but I knew I wasn't going back to where I was coming

The Garden of My Soul

from, Like the Father of faith, Abraham, I was obeying God, one step at a time. One instruction at a time even if I was holding my breath because it felt like I was free falling. Deep down, I knew God had me.

In the midst of all of that, my fiancé wanted us to get married in 2012. If you know my husband, he was determined and intentional from the beginning. He wasn't put off by what some would call "the drama", he loved me and my daughter, showed care, took responsibility even when we were just dating.

So, when he came with marriage, I guess it was like wow, too fast. Could it really be this quick? These were the things I longed for when I was in dysfunction, these were the things I prayed for but now it felt surreal, scary and maybe I felt can this really be trusted.

I told my fiancé and Bishop that I wanted to do things in order and preferred to get married after I graduated. It just felt like I wanted to give myself what everyone else had. You know, go to university and then get married. I had done many things upside down prior and wanted order and normalcy.

My Bishop and husband reassured me that God's time is God's time no matter what I am doing which encouraged me to be at peace with the decision to start planning the wedding. Besides, the ship had sailed on me trying to be like everyone else, I wasn't everyone

The Garden of My Soul

else and my path was not going to be like everyone else. And I finally started getting used to that and seeing the beauty in my story.

A couple of weeks before my wedding day, I went back to Selfridges for a facial, and on the way to the facial department, I popped by to see my work colleagues as I hadn't seen them in a long time. I bumped into another lady who worked at another concession. Whilst catching up with her, I asked her where they moved my old department to which she stated that the department was shut down and everyone was made redundant.

That was a light bulb moment – confirmation of another turning point in my life where I knew that my walk with God was and will continue to be built on trust – a trusted relationship where I can't always assess the physical circumstance to navigate the future. I can't always do what seems logical if I wanted to step into all God had for me. It's all about walking by FAITH and not by sight.

Keep planting good seeds because though your beginnings are small, your latter end shall greatly increase. Allow the Holy Spirit to work on your wound's day by day. These come in stages, and I've not seen a gardener only work on their garden in a day. It is a step-by-step and continuous process which the Lord has inspired me to share with you.

The Garden of My Soul

But God's intention requires your action; FAITH! To see God's promises, we have to be ready to work! How much do you desire freedom from the same cycle? For me to be where I am today, I had to put in the work, step out in faith and walk on the water just like Peter did in **Matthew 14:22-33 (NLT)** which says:

(22) "Immediately after this, Jesus insisted that His disciples get back into the boat and cross to the other side of the lake, while He sent the people home.

(23) After sending them home, He went up into the hills by Himself to pray. Night fell while He was there alone.

(24) Meanwhile, the disciples were in trouble far away from the land, for a strong wind had risen, and they were fighting heavy waves.

(25) About three o'clock in the morning, Jesus came towards them walking on the water.

(26) When the disciples saw Him walking on the water, they were terrified. In their fear, they cried out 'It's a ghost!'

(27) But Jesus spoke to them at once. 'Don't be afraid,' He said. 'Take courage. I am here!'

(28) Then Peter called to Him, 'Lord, if it's really you, tell me to come to you, walking on the water.'

The Garden of My Soul

(29) 'Yes, come' Jesus said. So, Peter went over the side of the boat and walked on the water towards Jesus.

(30) But when he saw the strong wind and the waves, he was terrified and began to sink. 'Save me, Lord!' he shouted.

(31) Jesus immediately reached out and grabbed Him. 'You have so little faith' Jesus said. 'Why did you doubt me?'

(32) When they climbed back into the boat, the wind stopped.

(33) Then the disciples worshiped Him. 'You really are the Son of God!' they exclaimed."

This scripture is so powerful! I want to focus in on the fact that Peter wasn't the only one on the boat.

However, Peter *was* the only one brave enough and tenacious to step out of the boat. He had faith in Jesus. I am sure when Peter began to step out of the boat, the disciples looked at him as if he was mad. This is exactly how I felt when I stepped out in faith by leaving Selfridges whilst other people stayed on the boat where they were comfortable. In the natural, no one can walk on water so Peter wasn't really walking on water, he was walking on the words Jesus spoke to him; "Come!"

The Garden of My Soul

I knew that my trust couldn't be in the boat. It couldn't be in my part time job, it couldn't be in the welfare system. I was going to say I couldn't remain comfortable, but truth is I wasn't comfortable, it wasn't a comfort zone. All I had learnt was survival. So, I gave up barely surviving and put my faith and confidence comes in Jesus.

Stepping out is a *very* uncomfortable experience. It makes you feel so vulnerable, however, stepping out in faith can lead you to experience unusual demonstrations of God's Power. Peter's faith began to deteriorate when he realised what he was doing. I am not talking about walking on water.

Your water may represent different challenges in life which is where you must keep your eyes on the One that can help you and not on the waves in difficult situations. The moment you decide to reject what the devil tries to make your norm, all hell will break loose, but you have to keep your eyes on Jesus Christ and what He said to you.

If you have received Jesus into your life, know that the challenges you are facing is not evidence that you are being rejected by God, or being punished. The devil is just angry so make sure you arm yourself with the truth. Know that whatever hardship you may encounter during this journey will produce something good in you.

Check out the truth below:

The Garden of My Soul

Romans 5:1-5 (NLT):

(1) "Therefore, since we have been made right in God's sight by faith, we have peace with God because of what Jesus Christ our Lord has done for us.

(2) Because of our faith, Christ has brought us into this place of undeserved privilege where we now stand and we confidently and joyfully look forward to sharing God's glory.

(3) We can rejoice, too, when we run into problems and trials, for we know that they help us develop endurance.

(4) And endurance develops strength of character, and character strengthens our confident hope of salvation.

(5) And this hope will not lead to disappointment. For we know how dearly God loves us, because He has given us the Holy Spirit to fill our hearts with His love."

We rejoice when we run into problems not because we deny its tragedy, but because going through trails is what is strengthens our character; that's if we are willing to learn from them. We must learn from our mistakes and challenges. Instead of just going through choose to grow through in order to move forward.

There are many people who are still sitting the same exams and going through the same mountain because

The Garden of My Soul

they refuse to grow from their mistakes and challenges. I don't know about you but for me, I was tired of going through the same mountains of being fed up. Many believers have taken their eyes away from Christ, merely trying to ride above the waves in their own strength, whilst others have become tired and given up.

When someone makes an attempt to swim in the middle of the ocean, if the waves are aggressive and moving with speed, that person will become tired and eventually drown. This is what many people experience from time to time; they are trying to survive the waves and becoming weary but take heart; our problems help us to develop perseverance.

Make sure you carry these four words: "I'm not giving up" when things get hard, or you run into problems that cause delay. We keep going; we don't stop! During the process, our character is also being developed as we go through the journey with Christ. Our relationship with God is deepened which makes us hopeful for the future knowing that the Lord who brought us out of our situations will do it again; He will not fail.

The Garden of My Soul

Journal Section:

On the journal section below, write the vision for your life and pray over it. Ask the Lord to reveal the plans He has for your life and all you desire to accomplish whether they are short or long-term goals. Keep sowing good seeds towards it and one day it *will* manifest.

As you write down your desires, understand that they must be in alignment with the Word of God. For example, desiring another man's wife or another woman's husband isn't something that God will ordain. Ask God for your own spouse according to His Will for your life below:

Habakkuk 2:2-3 (KJV):
(2) "And the Lord answered me and said, 'Write the vision and make it plain upon tablets that he may run that readeth it.

(3) For the vision is yet for an appointed time, but at the end it shall speak and not lie. Though it tarry, wait for it because it will surely come; it will not tarry.'"

Ponder on the vision for your life. This is the first step towards your future. Seeing your vision on paper will motivate and encourage you to keep going and trusting in the promise. We can begin to imagine the great things that God will have us to do and the future that's ahead of us.

The Garden of My Soul

Additional notes/key scripture:

The Garden of My Soul

The Garden of My Soul

Short-term goals:
Where do you see God leading you within the next year or two?

_____
_____
_____
_____
_____
_____
_____
_____
_____
_____
_____
_____
_____
_____
_____
_____
_____
_____
_____
_____

The Garden of My Soul

Additional notes/key scripture:

The Garden of My Soul

Long-term goals:
Where do you see God leading you for the future?

The Garden of My Soul

Additional notes/key scripture:

The Garden of My Soul

CHAPTER SEVEN

Back to Eden

This life will never be perfect. We live in a fallen world; seasons change as we know. They include winter, autumn, spring and summer. We will have our ups and our downs as the Lord said in **John 16:33 (NIV)**: *"I have told you these things, so that in Me you may have peace. In this world you will have trouble but take heart! I have overcome the world."* I want to thank God that He has set me free from all my past pain. Am I still a work in progress? Of course, I am. I've moved on with my life and continue to keep the fruits of the Holy Spirit by the grace of God.

My relationship with my daughter has been restored because in hindsight, I felt as if I experienced a loss of innocence as I didn't get to be a child. To be transparent, I didn't enjoy being a parent for a long time. I loved my daughter to the moon and back, but the responsibilities I had were difficult. Don't get me wrong I was still there for her, I loved her, she was my handbag, she went everywhere with me. I tried to shield her from the fact I wasn't enjoying it but I am so glad we both got through that season.

Now it's different; God has enabled me to embrace my two daughters and I am enjoying the season of being the best mother I can be. It's humbling to know

The Garden of My Soul

that God has entrusted me to look after them. I can testify that the Lord took me back to how the garden of Eden was before the fall.

This book started over 10 years ago, but the Lord asked me to release it now. In that time, many things happened. Firstly, my husband and I have been married for over eight years. Tayah has grown into such a beautiful teenager. I also have another beautiful daughter with my husband. Guess what her name is? Eden! Remember Eden means pleasure, and she really does bring more joy to the family and has a lot of energy! The Lord has brought me so far and I am amazed at His love and mercy every day. I was told I couldn't attend university as a single mother, but to the glory of God, I am a graduate with one bachelor's degree and two masters. I am a business studies teacher and I run a wedding business and ministry with my husband.

Also, I can now add that I'm the author of this book you are reading to the glory of God. What's amazing is that God isn't done with me yet. There are many more projects to come by the Grace of God! I don't say all of this to boast, but like Apostle Paul, if I boast, I boast only in my heavenly Father, my Saviour, Jesus Christ. I can honestly say that God can change your story, and if He did it for me, He can and will surely do it for you too! He is no respecter of persons and shows no favouritism. What a great God we serve, loving, caring and a respecter of every individual.

The Garden of My Soul

CHAPTER EIGHT

The Message

To be very transparent, there's no particular formula I can give to help you. All I know is that God can change your life. I can't give you a date or time when my life changed. It just changed as I remained consistent by staying in His Word. I remained planted in church and open to God with a sincere heart allowing Him to mould and shape me. On top of all of that, I practically positioned myself for change.

Through experience, one thing you can't do when dealing with wounds of the past is to self-medicate. Many people self-medicate their pain through gambling, sex, drugs, alcohol, and the list goes on.

I was there. I did it and tried it but it wasn't fulfilling. The problem with self-medicating is that it doesn't last long, and in turn leads to addiction. It is equivalent to cutting the top surface of the weeds and not pulling them out from the roots. The issue is never gambling; the issue is never sex, the issue is never drugs, but the issue is pain and dealing with it head on.

The Garden of My Soul

When I was a single mother, I never wanted to stay at home. My daughter either used to go to her dad's house at the weekends or a family member that wanted her around. When she was gone, I never stayed at home because I knew countless thoughts would have sprung through my mind.

I had the *Martha spirit*; always wanting to be out and busy which was when I would self-medicate in the form of dating men, going out with my friends, or staying at someone else's house for fear of being alone. What I really needed was to get before God and open up my heart and invest time with Him.

Sometimes, the enemy will put shame around what we reveal to God. There are issues we need to bring to God; however, the enemy would prefer that we stay silent. Looking back, I didn't speak about my issues in depth to anyone until one day, I was chosen to speak at my friend Sarah's event and was being asked a few questions about my past and the domestic violence I experienced.

From nowhere, I broke down weeping. After the tears stopped, I felt somewhat embarrassed because at the time, I didn't know where it came from. The weeds started showing up and the wounds from the past. Even though I shared a part of my story with the audience, it did eventually enable me to heal within as it was part of my deliverance, and I believe as we open up to God and to the right people, we will feel a sense of freedom.

The Garden of My Soul

During the gardening process, several strategies are put in place to stop pests from coming in. We can apply these strategies for when our spiritual lives are being attacked. One approach I utilised when my husband first met me was to guard my heart as I was fearful of being hurt again and wanted to make sure the man coming into my life was God's Will for me.

I was tired of depending on myself and decided to lean on God for His guidance. I tried not to get too emotionally attached to him which came across as if I was playing hard to get. Before I knew it, he was already speaking to me about marriage. I felt as if things were moving too fast, but it was God's timing. When I fully let go, that was when God took the wheel and started stirring it towards the right direction.

I want to remind you to stop nursing and rehearsing the sins of the past because when you do, you are poisoning yourself.

We can learn a great lesson from the story of Joseph in Genesis 37 to chapter 45 who innocently told his brothers a dream which made them get offended and sold him. From that point forward, Joseph went through many trials and tribulations because of his brothers, however, he ended up becoming very successful.

When he had the power to get even with his brothers, he chose not to. Instead, he showed them mercy and didn't blame them. He knew God had turned his pain

The Garden of My Soul

into purpose and positioned him to save them from famine. When you truly heal, revenge is far from your mind, you can even use your freedom to help those that once hurt you. You may think that is farfetched but trust me, revenge brings you to their level.

When you heal, you operate in the realm of God who makes the sun to rise on the good and the evil and causes it to rain on the righteous and the unrighteous. (Mathew 5:45). Holding unforgiveness harms you, but you have the power to let go. Don't allow your mind to be tortured by what other people have done or how they have treated you.

There are people I could hold hostage in my heart; however, I've decided to move forward and make the right decisions that will benefit my future. I cannot change or control anyone, neither can I force anyone that's caused me pain to say those desired words we want to hear such as: "I'm sorry." I can only change who I am because when I change, the world around me changes too.

When you see life from a positive perspective, it helps a lot, and now, I look through the lenses of compassion instead of assuming their hurt for me is intentional. It's good to be able to understand other people's hurt as they express it through their words, and this could be for various reasons such as not having parents that showed them love or going through multiple seasons of stress.

The Garden of My Soul

This is just a way to help yourself by understanding that hurt people, hurt people. Think about the people you've hurt along the way.

In the same way you want to be shown mercy, you should also extend mercy to others just as the Lord does forgiving us of our sins daily. God's Word contains His Will for us, and this includes how we think that is constantly being influenced by the power of the Holy Spirit. We must learn how to renew and transform our minds daily and make a conscious decision to study the Word and pray whilst targeting the areas of weakness. For example, if you struggle with rejection, pull out those weeds of negative thinking and replace them with the truth by reading scriptures about the love of God.

God will never leave nor forsake you; He is a faithful God. Don't just read that He is faithful but put your faith to the test until you start living in acts of faith. In Psalm 19:7 it says, "the instructions of the Lord are perfect, reviving the soul." The word of God is powerful that when you read it, your soul starts to change and transform through the Holy Spirit, as you allow Him to speak within you and making the Word be a part of you.

Allow the Holy Spirit to work in you, for He knows everything. The Bible says in Jeremiah 1:5 (AMP): *"Before I formed you in the womb, I knew you and approved of you as My chosen instrument, and before*

The Garden of My Soul

you were born, I consecrated you to Myself as My own; I have appointed you as a prophet to the nations."

We are responsible for our own gardens. All the tools are available to us, but it's what we do with them that matters. The Word of God is available to us in various formats through the internet, audio-bibles and various bible apps on our phones.

I love what Jeremiah 1:10 says:

"See, I have this day appointed you to the oversight of the nations and of the kingdoms to root out and pull down, to destroy and to overthrow, to build and to plant."

Did you read that properly? You can't plant seeds if the weeds are occupying that space, it won't grow or stand strong.

You have to destroy every negative weed before you plant the good seed. Sometimes, there are areas in our lives we have been working on where we see gradual change, and therefore, it should be celebrated. Don't beat yourself up about the changes you are not seeing but keep putting your hand to the plough because in due season, you shall reap a reward if you do not give up.

The Garden of My Soul

By maintaining your garden, you have to decide to make right decisions. I've made numerous wrong decisions in my earlier years of life, but now I know better, I get to make the right decisions moving forward. I remember hearing my Bishop saying these words: 'Anyone can make decisions in life, but you can't choose the consequences.' This is so true as the decisions I made is what I am facing today which a lot of young people aren't aware of.

Young people don't realise that the decisions they make today will impact them later in the future which could lead to regret and frustration. I felt this for many years, and I knew even though God had changed my life, I'd still have to face the consequence of the decisions I made. It won't just disappear, and this is why we have to understand the importance of making the right decisions in life.

I want you to understand that failure will not get the last word, however, if you have made wrong decisions, ensure that you recognise them and repent.

Be realistic so that you don't stay in the place of failure. When we understand this and abandon our previous behaviours, God can still use us, and our lives will change for His Glory. This is something I had to accept to move on with my life. A decision I made to get into a serious relationship at a young age led me growing up too soon. By the time I got to the age where I met my husband, I couldn't fully enjoy

The Garden of My Soul

my marriage because I felt as if I was responsible for my past mistakes; instead of me enjoying that season, I despised it. I didn't at the time embrace the seasons of going on holidays with friends, travelling around the world, socialising and enjoying my youth.

I decided not to focus 100% in school or college, so the consequence of that was not meeting the university's criteria and had to go back to adult college and retake Maths. I then started going to university later than expected which impacted my family by not having enough finances saved which affected school weekend activities for our daughter, to going through a season where when our car would break down, we could not afford it. It was certainly not easy, however, my husband and I had to keep our heads held high.

During the early years our marriage, we were supposed to be travelling and starting together financially however, it was a challenge to have that experience as I was still at university. My family had to carry the burden of the decisions I made many years ago, which bought stress to my family. The finances I had in the past that was meant to be saved for rainy days was spent unwisely because it made me feel good at the time, but it led to bills being missed and ultimately being in a lot of debt which was challenging to get out of.

Decisions are crucial and in Deuteronomy 30:19, it says **"This day, I call the heavens and the earth as**

The Garden of My Soul

witnesses against you, that I have set before you life and death, blessings and curses. Now choose life, so that you and your children may live."

We are free to make choices every day, however, we can't choose the consequences. David committed adultery with someone else's wife, and even though God forgave him, the baby still died. Deuteronomy highlights that the choices we make in life doesn't only impact us, but our children and the next generation. I not only have a passion for those who have gone through life's challenges, but for young people. When you are young, you believe that you know everything, and the focus is on short term gains and not long-term wisdom for living.

I hope this book has encouraged you, especially the young women to think twice before making certain decisions because it can impact your future. Put in the work now and be focused so you can relax and enjoy the future.

Do not allow emotions to make decisions for you because as quickly as emotions come, they will leave you stranded with regret. If you are in a position where you have already made decisions that have left you scarred, remember that there is hope; I am a living testimony of that! My journey shows you that it doesn't matter what you've done in the past; your life's adventure is not over. God is at work reclaiming your story and isn't done with you, so don't give up. Failure doesn't disqualify you. It did not disqualify

The Garden of My Soul

me from being used, neither did it disqualify me from making the choices to change the trajectory of my life. I choose to celebrate my everyday small wins, whether it is changes in my character, a change in my mindset, or a change in career progression; I choose to change my perspective and celebrate every progress and I pray you do the same starting from today.

Journal Section:

Write down what you will be changing from today:

_____
_____
_____
_____
_____
_____
_____
_____
_____
_____
_____
_____
_____

The Garden of My Soul

Additional notes/key scripture:

I want you to acknowledge those that haven't known or given their lives to Christ. Where I am today would not have been possible on my own. I was led to repeat a few words by a sweet lady on the bus in Hackney and look at me today. Jesus changed me because I gave my life to Him. My life was and still is in His hands. If you aren't born again, you are still in sin because of what Adam and Eve did in the Garden of Eden.

Our natural state is that we are sinners and have all fallen short of the Glory of God. The Bible says in Romans 6:23 that: *"The wages of sin is death, but the gift of God is eternal life through Jesus Christ."* Even though we have sinned and deserve death, God gave us the gift of His son Jesus Christ to die for us so we wouldn't have to live eternity in hell.

The Garden of My Soul

For this reason, I want you to say the following prayer out loud from your heart. This is the best decision you will ever make in your entire life; to become born again. Speak these words out loud:

"Dear Jesus,
I know that I have sinned against You
I confess that I am a sinner
I accept the sacrifice You made on the Cross on my behalf, I believe that you died for me, and you rose again.
I ask You to come into my heart
Please cleanse me from my sins and give me eternal life
I repent from my sins and put my trust in You, in Jesus' Name, Amen."

If you've said this prayer from your heart, that's it! You are born again! Congratulations! Now all you need to do is buy yourself a Bible and find a Holy Spirit-filled church to establish yourself in and your Father in heaven shall lead you in Jesus' Name, Amen. You are more than welcome to attend Salem International Christian Centre.
Email: salemeurope.org.

For more information on our social media platforms, follow us on:

Instagram: taramulumba1, journeyofalifetime13 and warriorwives07

The Garden of My Soul

References and Key Term Definitions

- Definition of *the perfect garden* –
  "A garden is a planned space, usually outdoors, set aside for the display, cultivation and enjoyment of plants and other forms of nature,"
  <https://en.wikipedia.org/wiki/Garden>

- Indiana Department of Health: "Research states that rodents try to find nesting areas where they hide under rubbish, timber, wood, in drain pipes or under sheds,"
  <https://www.in.gov/isdh/23256.htm>

- Plant Definition on Google: "Planting means to place a seed, bulb, or plant in the ground so that it can grow."

- Rodents Definition on Google: "Rodents are not wanted in a garden because of the damage they cause to the fruits, seeds, vegetables, bulbs and plants. Rodents can also expose people and pets to various diseases,"
  <https://www.rentokil.co.uk/rodents/rodents-in-the-garden/>

- Swanee Definition: "The meaning and origin of the phrase 'down the Swanee' – The colloquial phrase down the Swanee means

The Garden of My Soul

completely lost or wasted; synonymous phrases: down the pan – down the toilet – down the tube(s) – down the plughole – down the drain – down the gurgler," <https://wordhistories.net/2019/11/29/down-swanee/>

- Urine definition: "Can burn the roots of the plants," <https://goveganic.net/Fertilizing-with-human-urine> and <https://theconversation.com/curious-kids-why-do-leaves-fall-off-trees-111914>

Printed in Great Britain
by Amazon